The Royal Exhibition Building, Melbourne

A Guide

Elizabeth Willis

museum
VICTORIA

Cover: Eastern facade of the
Exhibition Building, c. 1901.

Source: National Library of Australia

Cover inset pictures, left to right:
The Exhibition Building.
Illustrated Australian News, 9 October 1880.

Source: State Library of Victoria

Long view of the Royal Exhibition Building.

Source: Museum Victoria

Interior of the Royal Exhibition Building.

Photographer: Peter Mappin
Source: Museum Victoria

Pages ii and iii: Interior of the Royal Exhibition
Building featuring dome and arches.

Photographer: James Lauritz
Source: Museum Victoria

Published by Museum Victoria, 2004
© Text copyright Museum Victoria 2004
© Images copyright Museum Victoria unless otherwise noted

We have made every effort to obtain copyright and moral permission
for use of all images. Please advise us of any errors or omissions.

Australian Society and Technology Department
Museum Victoria
GPO Box 666E
Melbourne
Victoria 3001
Australia
(03) 8347 1111

www.museum.vic.gov.au

Chief Executive Officer: Dr J. Patrick Greene

Director, Collections, Research and Exhibitions:
Dr Robin Hirst

Head, Australian Society and Technology Department:
Dr Richard Gillespie

Author: Elizabeth Willis

Text editor: David Hudson
Designer: Luisa Laino

National Library of Australia
Cataloguing-in-Publication Data:
Willis, Elizabeth, 1947–.
    The Royal Exhibition Building, Melbourne: a guide.

    ISBN 0 9577471 4 4.

    1. Royal Exhibition Building (Melbourne, Vic.) – History.
    2. Royal Exhibition Building – (Melbourne, Vic.) – Guidebooks.
    3. Exhibition buildings – Victoria – Melbourne – Guidebooks.
    I. Museum Victoria

381.1099451

Contents

Foreword

In most great cities there is one building that epitomises its spirit and history. It may be a cathedral, a palace, a town hall or a parliament. In Melbourne it is undoubtedly the Royal Exhibition Building. From 1880 its dome, inspired by the Duomo in Florence, dominated the city skyline. In 1880, and again in 1888, the international exhibitions it housed had a profound impact on the citizens of a city that had existed only half a century. The building proclaimed to the world that Melbourne was an international city, with the wealth to spend on lavish display. The content of the exhibitions also had a transforming effect as the people of Victoria were brought face to face with the latest manufactures from all over the globe, raising their expectations of what might be possible for them. They came in huge numbers: 1.3 million visits were made to the 1880 International Exhibition and 2 million visits in the five months that the Centennial Exhibition was staged.

For many exhibition buildings, the end of the exhibition movement marked the end of their useful lives; they were demolished or decayed, or caught fire and were burnt to the ground. Remarkably, the Royal Exhibition Building in its garden setting has survived virtually intact, although at times its survival has been threatened. In this guidebook you will find vivid descriptions of the great exhibitions and fascinating information on other activities that the building has accommodated. These range from the first federal parliament to Ideal Home shows, influenza hospital to a place for peace and religious rallies, examination hall to venue for Olympic wrestling. There has always been a mix of grand occasions and popular entertainment in the Royal Exhibition Building.

Today the Royal Exhibition Building is part of Museum Victoria, together with the Melbourne Museum that stands alongside it, the Immigration Museum and Scienceworks. It continues to play a leading role in the life of Melbourne, housing exhibitions, concerts, religious services, banquets, university exams and meetings. Visitors can enjoy guided tours of the building and explore the beautiful Carlton Gardens that surround it. They can also discover Melbourne's nineteenth-century grandeur on the Golden Mile trail. The gardens and the Exhibition Building have been nominated for inscription on UNESCO's World Heritage List. Great international exhibitions were a phenomenon of the nineteenth century that helped create the culture of the industrial age that crossed frontiers and bridged oceans. As the best surviving example of its type, the Royal Exhibition Building has become not only the symbol of Melbourne but a structure of global significance.

Dr J. Patrick Greene
Chief Executive Officer
Museum Victoria

Chronology of the Royal Exhibition Building

1851 **The Great Exhibition, London**
This heralds the age of the international exhibitions. Melbourne holds trade exhibitions in 1854, 1861, 1866–67, 1872–73, 1875 and 1879–80.

1877 **Architects begin work**
Melbourne architects Reed and Barnes are commissioned to design a large exhibition hall in the Carlton Gardens. Construction begins in 1879.

1880–81 **The Melbourne International Exhibition**
The first show in the new building attracts 1.3 million visitors. Annexes run north of the building to the park boundaries.

1884 **'Salvos' celebrate**
Ten thousand people attend a rally for the first anniversary of the Melbourne Salvation Army.

1885 **The Aquarium opens**
It also contains an ethnographic display and several historical tableaux.

1886 **Supporting charities**
The Chinese community hold a pageant and performance in aid of the Women's Hospital.

1888–89 **The Centennial International Exhibition**
This enormous exhibition runs for five months, attracts 2 million visitors, but operates at a loss.

1889 **The Australian Natives' Association**
This society organises its first Foundation Day Fete, on 26 January, the anniversary of European settlement of Australia.

1891 **Art and music**
A Picture Gallery, Museum and fernery are added to the Aquarium, and promenade concerts are held in the Great Hall.

1901 **Parliament opens**
The first Australian federal parliament opens on 9 May. The Victorian parliament meets in an annexe to the building, 1901–27.

1905 **'Buy Australian'**
The first 'All-Australian' exhibition is held to promote Australian manufactured goods. It is sponsored by the Australian Natives' Association.

1907 **Promoting women's work**
The first Australian Exhibition of Women's Work attracts 16 000 entries.

1912 **The motor age**
The first Motor Show is held in the building.

1919 **Housing the sick**
A temporary hospital is established in the building, to cope with the Spanish influenza epidemic.

1922 **Remembering the war**
The Australian War Museum (later to become the Australian War Memorial) opens in the building on Anzac Day, 25 April.

1930 **Feeding the hungry**
Sidney Myer, merchant and philanthropist, provides a free Christmas Day dinner for 11 000 people.

1936 **The suburban dream**
The first Ideal Home Exhibition is held in the building.

1941   Men in Air Force Blue
The RAAF School of Technical Training occupies the building until 1946.

1947   The age of chemistry
The Chemex exhibition displays the new technology of plastic compounds.

1948   A white elephant?
Members of the Melbourne City Council propose that the building should be demolished and replaced by government offices. The proposal is narrowly defeated.

1949   Receiving migrants
A migrant reception centre is established in the grounds; it remains until 1962.

1949   Homes for the future
The Red Cross Modern Home Exhibition includes architect Robin Boyd's 'House of Tomorrow'.

1950   Seeking peace
Ten thousand people at the Australian Peace Congress hear Anglican priest Dr Hewlett Johnson (the 'Red Dean') warn of the danger of nuclear war.

1952   Dancing the night away
The Royale Ballroom opens and becomes a popular meeting spot.

1953   A major loss
The Aquarium and most of the exhibits are destroyed by fire.

1956   The Melbourne Olympics
Competitions in weightlifting and wrestling are held in the building. A new annexe is built for the basketball competition.

1960s–present   A testing time
Thousands of students annually sit for school and university examinations in the Great Hall.

1975   Recognising the building's significance
The building is added to the Register of the National Estate.

1980   'Royal' at last!
The building is renamed the Royal Exhibition Building during a visit by Princess Alexandra.

1985–95   Restoration begins
The building's interior is restored to the decorative scheme of 1901.

1996   A new owner
The building and its archives come under the care of Museum Victoria. The annexes are demolished.

2001   Smarter than ever
The restoration of the northern exterior of the building is completed.

2003   Of world significance
The Royal Exhibition Building and the Carlton Gardens are considered for World Heritage listing.

'A Palace of Industry' for
'The Athens of the South'

1

The Royal Exhibition Building is a product of the optimism, enthusiasm and energy of the people of Melbourne in the late nineteenth century. In 1879, when the foundation stone was laid, Melbourne was an extremely prosperous city, basking in the wealth from the richest gold rush in the world. Nearly 200 million pounds worth of gold had been mined at Bendigo, Ballarat and other fields, and there seemed no end to new discoveries. Everywhere new buildings were going up, overseas investment was growing, the stock market was booming; the colony of Victoria had the highest rate of home ownership in the world, and Victorians were earning some of the highest wages in the world. Melbourne, founded in 1835, had become a capital city of over 260 000 people in fewer than 50 years. The future seemed unlimited, and Victorians wanted to make sure that their achievements and the opportunities they presented were publicised throughout the world. How better to do this than by organising and hosting a world fair, an international exhibition?

The first international exhibition was London's Great Exhibition of 1851 in the Crystal Palace, and it was quickly followed by similar events in Dublin, New York, Paris and other centres. International exhibitions served as showcases for the natural resources of the colonial world, and for the ingenuity and technological achievements of the machine age. Visitors thronged to see the exotic and the new,

The Royal Exhibition Building and Carlton Gardens in autumn.
Source: Museum Victoria

to wonder at evidences of ancient civilisations and to admire the marvels of new inventions like the typewriter and the gramophone. The exhibitions brought people and objects from all parts of the industrialising world together; they became venues for the transfer of ideas as well as of information about new materials and technologies.

Since its beginnings, Victorians had been enthusiastic participants in the world fair movement. Three years after London's exhibition, Melbourne held an 'Exhibition of Produce and Works of Industry' in a purpose-built pavilion in La Trobe Street, and in 1855 the colony sent a significant exhibit, including a substantial collection of gold nuggets, to the Exposition Universelle in Paris. Several local and intercolonial exhibitions were held in a new hall, behind the State Library, during the 1860s and 1870s, and exhibits were sent to exhibitions in London, 1862, Paris, 1867, Philadelphia, 1876 and London, 1886, among others. The manufacturers of Victoria, who were increasing in wealth and influence under the government's policies of protection for local industry, were keen to show off the variety of goods produced in the colony, and lobbied the government to support a truly international exhibition.

If Melbourne was going to host an international exhibition, it had to do it properly. In 1878 the government agreed to finance a new Exhibition Building, on a site close to the omnibus route in Nicholson Street, just on the outskirts of the central city. A committee of merchants and public men was formed and began planning for a large international exhibition in 1880. They organised an architectural competition for the erection of the new exhibition building. It was won by Joseph Reed, of the firm Reed and Barnes, who were also responsible for several other Melbourne landmarks, including the Independent Church in Collins Street and the Town Hall.

Reed's was a grand design, influenced by *Rundbogenstil,* a round-arched architectural style combining elements from Byzantine, Romanesque, Lombardic and Italian Renaissance buildings. The design of the dome was influenced by Brunelleschi's fifteenth century cathedral at Florence, and Reed also suggested that he was influenced by buildings in Normandy, Caen and Paris. He designed a main Great Hall, with two brick annexes and extensive temporary exhibition halls.

Above: The Exhibition Building under construction, 1879. This photograph, by Charles Nettleton, shows the timber interior of the dome.
Source: Royal Historical Society of Victoria

Below left: Unpacking exhibits in the Main Avenue at the Melbourne International Exhibition. *Illustrated Australian News,* 28 August 1880.
Source: State Library of Victoria

Below right: Some time after the building was completed, Charles Nettleton climbed to the top of the building and took this view of the new gardens.
Source: Museum Victoria

Governor Bowen laid the foundation stone in February 1879, and William Clarke, president of the commissioners and later to be knighted for his public work, expressed his pride in the project: 'The place where your Excellency will today lay the foundation stone of a Palace of Industry was within a generation part of an unknown forest, in an almost unknown land. It is now the site of a populous and well-built city, presenting all the evidences of wealth and civilisation, taking rank with the foremost cities of the world, and surpassing in many respects the capitals of ancient and powerful states'.

Despite some criticisms of the design, and some changes necessitated by increased costs, the first exhibitors were able to move in on the contract completion date in May 1880.

The Great Hall is built of brick, on a bluestone base. It is planned with long central naves and stunted transepts, wide side aisles on the ground floor and continuous galleries on the first floor. There are four triumphal entrance porticoes, one on each side. Natural light flows in through the octagonal drum and lantern of the dome, four sets of fanlights, the rows of clerestory windows above the upper galleries, and the large windows in the lower tier of the external walls. The outstanding feature of the vast area, the finely proportioned Florentine dome, is 67 metres high. At the time that it was built, the Great Hall was the largest building in Australia, and taller than any spire in the city.

At the 1880 Exhibition, the Great Hall comprised only one-tenth of the whole space. The two permanent brick annexes were both nearly as long as the Great Hall; there was a temporary exhibition hall 250 metres long and 150 metres wide, and other large wooden temporary annexes to accommodate late entries from countries like Austria, Great Britain and Germany. The total exhibition space was about nine hectares. Seven million bricks were used in the construction.

Joseph Reed, together with horticulturalist and designer William Sangster, redesigned the surrounding southern Carlton Gardens to complement the Great Hall. The original garden design by Edward La Trobe Bateman, based on a series of curvilinear paths, was replaced by an axial, more ceremonial layout. The main entrance on the southern, city side became the apex of the design. A level promenade was created along the front of the building, and a semi-circular space had

The Great Hall is the only surviving section of the original complex built in 1880. It is 152 metres long from east to west and has a ground floor area of 7000 square metres. The balcony provides another 4500 square metres of display space.

Source: Museum Victoria

as its centrepiece an ornate fountain. A ceremonial approach was provided by a 24-metre wide avenue lined with plane trees. The *Argus* reported that in the centre of the avenue was a 'sward of buffalo grass in imitation of the *Tapis Vert* of Versailles'. Two other tree-lined paths were carved out to form a radiating axis from the fountain. There were two lakes, built to serve as reservoirs in case of fire, and new trees including Norfolk pines, elms, Moreton Bay figs and palm trees were planted. The promenade was lined with parterre flower beds in geometric shapes, closely planted with blue lobelias, scarlet geraniums, golden erythrium and blue and red verbenas. The effect was not entirely successful: one observer suggested that the garden beds looked like 'so many jam tarts or loud patterned hearth rugs fastened together'. This was the first use of bedding plants in Melbourne's public gardens and, despite the gaudiness, it helped create a new suburban fashion for densely planted and brightly coloured flower gardens.

The commissioners promoted the exhibition tirelessly in Europe and America. To their delight, bookings for space were soon flooding in; entries were eventually received from 33 nations. Months before the opening, enormous wooden containers filled with machines, pianos and other exhibits began arriving at the port of Melbourne. They were transported by flat-bed lorries to goods entrances in Nicholson and Rathdowne streets, and then winched onto tramways which extended throughout the complex. In one week in early July, 900 cases arrived at the site. Only weeks before the exhibition opened, additional annexes were being erected to accommodate more entries. As is the way for exhibitions everywhere, the final touches were still being put in place on the last day.

The International Exhibition opened on 1 October 1880. It was a public holiday in Melbourne. Defence forces, trade unionists and the fire brigades, accompanied by nine brass bands, joined colonial governors and politicians in state carriages in a long procession along Collins and Spring streets to the southern entrance. Inside, the building was thronged with crowds of well-dressed people. The gentlemen were in suits and waistcoats, with gold watches and fobs much in evidence; the ladies wore long brightly coloured dresses that swished over the wooden floor. They heard speeches, cheered Queen Victoria, sang the national anthem and the *Hallelujah Chorus,* and listened to an hour-long choral work celebrating the development and potential of Victoria.

The excited crowd included many who had immigrated during the 1850s gold rush. They had seen Melbourne change from a scatter of wooden houses to a marvellous modern city. Their hearts swelled with pride because this world fair was going to make Melbourne a truly international city. The new Exhibition Building, the largest building in Australia, was a symbol of their confidence in the future.

The Dome Promenade

No visit to the Exhibition Building was complete without a trip to the dome promenade, 30 metres above the gallery space. During the 1880s, visitors paid threepence to see the best possible view of the city and its suburbs. On a clear day they could see for 50 miles around, past Government House to the ships, large and small, on Port Phillip Bay, and across the hazy distance to the blue Dandenongs in the east. In 1885, George Sala, a London journalist, tagged the growing city 'Marvellous Melbourne', and a visit to the dome allowed locals to check on the progress of the building works around the booming city.

Overlooking Melbourne
from the Exhibition Building.
Australasian Sketcher,
19 June 1880.
Source: State Library of Victoria

The German beer cellar
spilled out from the basement
during the Centennial Exhibition.
Source: State Library of Victoria

Women in long skirts joined men and children in climbing the 80 steep steps to the external promenade around the dome. Some even clambered up the metal ladder on the exterior of the dome for a better view. The climb was well worth it. A visitor described how 'At one's feet lies the city, with its well-planned and equally well-executed streets, its commendable buildings, its domes, its churches and its towers. Then the suburbs, green almost as the country beyond and the waters of Port Phillip … The sight was grand enough to be subduing … and as we filed down the apparently endless stairs it was to the tune of silence'.

During the 1888 Centennial Exhibition, Waygood and Company installed a lift to the dome as a working exhibit. This was the first lift that many Victorians had travelled in. It carried over 127 000 people to see the view from the promenade; the cost was sixpence for adults and threepence for children.

It is hoped one day to reinstall the lift and promenade walk. Currently, only a select few – those who maintain the building and raise and lower the Australian flag on the top of the dome – have the opportunity to see the view. The central city has changed dramatically, but the view to the north, up Nicholson Street and across Fitzroy, still has the narrow lanes and crowded rows of terraces familiar to Melburnians a century ago.

The Basement

Under the floor of the Great Hall lies the basement, with its bluestone walls and long gloomy vistas. During the Centennial Exhibition, a cellar promoting German beer did a roaring trade here. It was also used for exhibits of wine and dairy products, and it became a temporary mortuary during the Spanish influenza epidemic of 1919. Now, it houses electrical and plumbing services, and there is a long central area of reinforced flooring, allowing heavy equipment to be used in the Great Hall without damaging the floor. Some curatorial departments of Museum Victoria, including Palaeontology and Mineralogy, are housed in the basement. It is an eerie experience now to stand in the damp area, conjure up the echoes of past visitors, and imagine the weight of the building bearing down upon you.

The Hochgurtel Fountain

The fountain in front of the Great Hall's southern entrance was designed in 1880 by Josef Hochgurtel, a recent immigrant from Cologne, and his colleague August Saupe. The Melbourne commissioners knew that grand fountains were essential elements of the best world fairs, and they wanted one that would display 'the power and grandeur of Melbourne's great water supply, the Yan Yean', opened in 1857 and still meeting the needs of the expanding metropolis in 1880.

Hochgurtel's fountain has four boys, representing the innocence and potential of youth, dancing around the central column. Above them are symbols of industry, commerce, science and art: a steam engine, sailing ship, telescope, surveying equipment, musical instruments, and a globe of the world. The fountain includes representations of the flora and fauna of Victoria, including platypuses, parrots and ferns, and, rather incongruously, what contemporaries described as 'crocodiles' – or are they goannas? The base of the fountain has three merpeople and several more young boys. The whole is made of Portland cement on a strong framework of stone and iron, and stands over 10 metres high.

Although the design was criticised for its confused iconography, the fountain has remained a focal point of the Carlton Gardens, and a favourite meeting place for people attending events in the Great Hall. It does not play in times of drought. In 1994, the fountain, which was badly corroded, was restored and repainted by the Melbourne City Council.

The Nicholson Street Entrance

The French fountain is the central feature of the flower garden near the Nicholson Street entrance. Three putti, winged children with dolphins on their heads, surround an urn which supports giant clam shells. There is an elegant acanthus leaf column that demonstrates the skill of nineteenth century craftsmen in the use of bronze for ornamentation. The fountain dates from the 1880 Exhibition, when it was originally installed as a centrepiece in the fernery, one of the quieter places at that event. French bronzes, vases, busts and statuary spilled outside the building almost to Nicholson Street, and the fountain seems to have been purchased by the trustees and erected here at the end of the exhibition.

Near the door is a bust of Louis Lawrence Smith (1830–1910), cantankerous politician, skilled surgeon and manufacturer of patent medicines, who was chair of the trustees of the Exhibition Building for 25 years. The bust was sculpted by Sir Edgar Bertram Mackennal, who also made the statue of King Edward VII in the Alexandra Gardens. It was paid for by public subscription and erected four years after Smith's death.

A column of Stawell stone stands defiantly at the corner of the building. It was erected in 1881 by John Woods, member for Stawell in the Victorian parliament, to show the durability of freestone from Mount Difficult, in his electorate. This material had been chosen for the west façade of Parliament House, but the first stone quarried from there was rejected by the contractors. Woods fought in a 'determined and persistent manner' for another trial of the stone, and was eventually successful.

Opposite: The Hochgurtel fountain stands at the top of the 'Grand Allée', the avenue of plane trees. The southern part of the Carlton Gardens was a pleasure garden and exhibition space during the great exhibitions.
Photographer: James Lauritz
Source: Museum Victoria

Above right: The French fountain today.
Source: Museum Victoria

Below right: The French fountain was a centre of attraction during the 1880 Exhibition.
Illustrated Australian News, 9 October 1880.
Source: State Library of Victoria

The International Exhibition of 1880–81

2

The Great Hall has been the scene of many events, but it was probably most crowded and most popular during the two international exhibitions, 1880–81 and 1888–89. The Melbourne International Exhibition of 1880–81 attracted more than 1.3 million people over eight months. The Carlton Gardens were the scene of trysts and assignations, gossip and introductions, as friends, families and lovers met to buy their tickets and stroll through the vast halls. Visitors came on foot through the gardens, by horse-drawn omnibuses along Nicholson Street, by hansom cab, by special trains from country districts, and by train and steamer from other colonies and from overseas.

There was always something new to see or do at the exhibition. When the delights of heavy industry and steam power waned, and the towers and pyramids of produce and manufactured goods had lost their charm, visitors could watch boiled sweets being made, sample the freshest of butter, and have the latest perfume sprayed on their handkerchief. They could wander through the Art courts, examining works from Great Britain as well as by local artists; they could admire or despise the craft work in the Ladies' court, or promenade gracefully along the upper galleries of the Great Hall and watch the crowd below. They could pause at the coffee and tea houses, the bars or the restaurants, to meet old friends and make new ones. The 1880 Exhibition was the first large event in Melbourne where young women of good family could go unchaperoned; they went to ogle, or be

Products on display in the Austrian court at the 1880 International Exhibition,
including tiles, decorative pottery and statuary for the home.

Photographer: Ludovico Hart
Museum Victoria Collection

Above: Crowds gather around the British exhibits of homewares under the dome at the Melbourne International Exhibition. *Official Record of the Melbourne International Exhibition, 1880–81.*

Museum Victoria Collection

Below: Brightly coloured glazed tiles, like these from Minton exhibited in 1880, influenced building styles in Victoria for the next 20 years.

Museum Victoria Collection

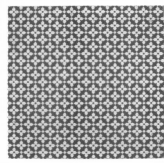

ogled by, young men and dapper exhibitors from all parts of the world. One young woman wrote in the visitors' book that it was 'a grand place to meet chaps' and various male visitors wrote that it was 'a good place for bachelors; the young Ladies were the best Exhibits'.

At one shilling for an adult ticket, entrance was within the reach of most people. The exhibition brought Victorians and visitors together in an event which blurred social boundaries. The *Illustrated Australian News* described the ritual of drinking tea in the Indian court: 'Thus we have old folks and young, the fashionable lady and the yokel, the colonial lad and the new chum, Sarah Jane and her young man, with Master Collingwood and Miss Fitzroy of larrikin notoriety, all mixed up together'. A wide range of souvenirs could be purchased. Many were made overseas, in Germany or Great Britain; these countries demonstrated new techniques of manufacture, such as microphotography. Visitors could buy a drinking glass etched with the newly fashionable ferns and engraved with their initials on the spot, or a medallion inscribed with the head of Queen Victoria on one side and on the other a scene of harvest plenty. Each day, a newspaper listing highlights of the day's events was printed on the premises, and several enterprising publishers took the opportunity to produce printed guides to Melbourne and Victoria. The Victorian government printed an official guide to the exhibition, and countries like Austria produced dual language catalogues of their exhibits.

The 1880 Exhibition was more than a social event; it had a serious purpose. Iron and steel goods, pharmaceuticals, jewellery, textiles, stationery, pipes, photographs, watches, scientific instruments, musical instruments, knives and other tools, wine, and samples of 'native industry' from the Pacific were all on display. The British court featured carpets, upholstery, chemicals, hardware, paperhangings, carriages, leathergoods and weighing machines; the Germans specialised in armaments and furniture, while the Americans offered agricultural machinery, barbed wire, typewriters, lawnmowers, cottons and electric lights. India, Mauritius, the Seychelles, Ceylon and the Straits Settlements showed natural products and craft, and models of ships and national costume. Manufacturers competed to be among the prize-winners, and a range of medals and certificates was produced for the successful exhibitors.

The Victorian court featured a large hanging shape, a rhombic dodecahedron representing the total quantity of gold obtained in the colony since 1851. There was a

Skilled craftsmen in West Bengal made a large group of clay 'Poonah figures', and dressed them in costumes representing different occupations and castes. These were exhibited in the Indian court in 1880, and then became part of the collection of Melbourne's Industrial and Technological Museum.

Museum Victoria Collection

This lawnmower, patented in 1880 and made by the Philadelphia Lawnmower Company, is similar to the prize-winning machine displayed at the International Exhibition.
Museum Victoria Collection

large display of models of mines and casts of nuggets, and the agricultural potential of Victoria was also promoted. In the Machinery annexe were several heavy locomotives, showing the colony's industrial manufacturing capability. For the organisers of the exhibition, this display vindicated the colony's policy of tariff protection for local manufacturers, and visitors commented that the New South Wales court, which featured largely primary products, looked undeveloped beside the Victorian exhibits.

From Europe, exhibitors of domestic wares showed off their latest products, which were for sale at the end of the exhibition. Melburnians began to fill their homes with imported hand-painted crockery, decorated ceramic tiles, cut glass and art porcelain. As Australian novelist Ada Cambridge wrote in 1903, the exhibition 'first taught us as a community the rudiments of modern art ... there is now no lack of what are generally described as artistic things ... but it was otherwise twenty years ago'.

Another exhibit that revolutionalised suburban life was the lawnmower shown in the American court. In the words of Robin Boyd, 'The model which won a diploma at the Melbourne Exhibition ... was efficient enough to remain unaltered for 70 years ... The amateur's lawnmower, as it was advertised, was cheap – and it changed the character of the garden. Now the poor man could have a croquet lawn finish to the grass around his house without the toil of scything and rolling'.

At the end of the exhibition, organisers had reason to be proud of their effort. Manufacturers and merchants from all over the world had visited Melbourne, and new trade links were being established with France and other parts of Europe. Both imports and exports were on the increase, and colonists were now hungry for new products. The historian Henry Giles Turner, writing 20 years after the event, described how Collins Street 'began to take on a cosmopolitan aspect' and claimed that 'much of the narrow provincialism of the colonists vanished'. A later historian has commented that the exhibition 'represents a monument to the optimism of the period, when it was still fervently believed that by the mutual spread of knowledge and the inter-change of culture, the world would be rapidly brought near the long-dreamed for Utopia'.

Most importantly, colonists had shown they could run a successful world fair. The exhibition had been a celebration of self-confidence, and it gave an enormous boost to the development of Australian nationalism.

Above: Certificates and medals were awarded in considerable numbers. This Award of Merit was presented to Professor McCoy of the National Museum of Victoria.

Museum Victoria Collection

Below left: This money-box, a cheap mass-produced item, was adapted to become a souvenir of the 1880 Exhibition.

Museum Victoria Collection

Below right: Gold and silver medallions were presented to successful exhibitors. Motifs included Queen Victoria and a laurel wreath of victory.

Museum Victoria Collection

Above: The Victorian court emphasised the colony's gold production. *Australasian Sketcher*, 6 November 1880.

Museum Victoria Collection

Below: The American court was initially rather bare as *Eric the Red*, the ship bringing material to Melbourne, was wrecked off the Victorian coast and most of the cargo was lost. However, the Americans sent another ship full of machines with potential for use in Australia, and visitors were enthralled by the latest examples of their ingenuity.

Photographer: Ludovico Hart
Museum Victoria Collection

Opposite: The manufacturers of Wertheim's sewing machines went to enormous trouble to present their product in an exotic pavilion.

Photographer: Ludovico Hart
Museum Victoria Collection

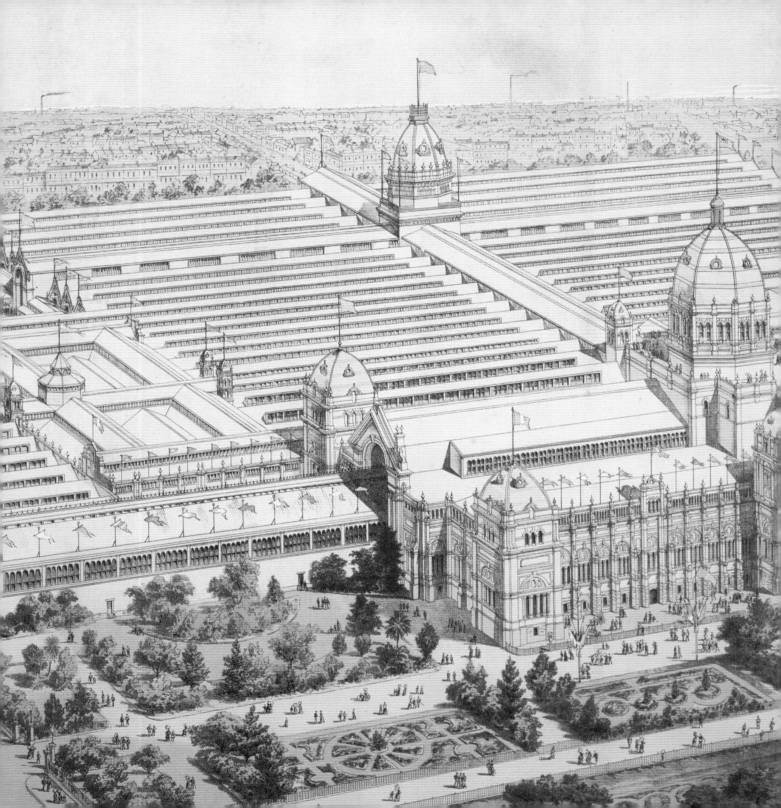

The Centennial Exhibition of 1888–89

3

The 1880 Exhibition was such a success that the merchants and politicians of Melbourne determined to do it all over again. Eight years later a new World Fair commemorated the centenary of the white settlement of Australia. Sydney, the site of the first European settlement, had erected an exhibition building in 1879, but it had burnt down three years later. New South Wales was therefore unable to host a world fair in 1888, but agreed to support the Victorian premier's proposal.

The Centennial Exhibition in Melbourne was huge. New temporary annexes (the ones from 1880 had been demolished) stretched to Carlton Street to the north, the exhibition halls covered almost 14 hectares of continuous roofed space, and nearly 2 million people came through the doors. Melbourne now had the largest building in the world under one roof. Nearly 40 countries sent exhibits, entering them in 92 separate categories.

The interiors of the exhibition halls were decorated with a new coloured scheme, designed by John Clay Beeler. This was the most flamboyant of the three schemes of 1880, 1888 and 1901; unfortunately, little of his work survives today. Up in the dome, on black outlined gold letters on a turquoise blue ground, was the text: *The earth is the Lord's and the fulness thereof.* Another motto, *Victoria welcomes all nations,* was painted over the north entrance to the main temporary annexe, the

Exhibition annexes took up all the northern part of the Carlton Gardens in 1888. *Australasian*, 4 August 1888.

Alice Chapman (1860–1929)
Gretchen, 1888
Oil on canvas

This work was exhibited in the Art court at the Centennial Exhibition, where it won a Certificate of Merit. The artist trained at the National Gallery School and was a member of the Victorian Artists' Society.

Museum Victoria Collection

Opposite: The Belgian Art Gallery at the Centennial Exhibition.

Source: National Library of Australia

Grand Avenue of Nations. Allegorical figures representing pioneers and explorers, Commerce, Science, Art and Music, and the four corners of the British Empire, decorated the walls around the dome.

Despite the rain, the opening procession on 1 August was watched by the greatest crowd Melbourne had known. Twenty bands provided the music, and nearly 1000 visiting seamen from the imperial fleet added formality to the parade of firemen, members of friendly societies in full regalia, and trade unionists marching behind their highly decorated banners. During the opening ceremony, a specially composed centennial cantata was sung by a choir of over 700 who invited guests to consider how 'Where the feet of the dark hunter strayed, [now] the wealth of the world is arrayed'.

For the first time, an international exhibition was open to the public at night. Electric lighting illuminated the interior displays and outlined the building's exterior. The curious could visit a specially erected building in the grounds to see the giant machines producing the electricity. Among the innovations on show for the first time were Edison phonographs, ice-making machines and diving apparatus. A large Armaments court displayed the latest technologies of war, including cannon and torpedoes. Another attraction was the Machinery annexe, which was much more interesting when the machinery was actually in motion. The *Argus* printing press produced 12 000 newspapers an hour, and there was a working dairy, as well as a large quartz-crushing stamper battery. The New South Wales court featured an enormous bust of Captain James Cook, treating him as the Father of Australia; the convict settlement of Sydney under Captain Arthur Phillip was ignored, even though the exhibition was meant to be celebrating the centenary of Phillip's arrival and the beginnings of European settlement. The Indigenous people of Australia, like the convicts, were largely ignored.

The French court included a model of the Eiffel Tower made out of champagne bottles; there were displays of Singer sewing machines in the American court, and 85 pianos in the German court. In the cellars in the basement, visitors could sample wines from Germany, France, Austro-Hungary, South Australia, New South Wales, Tasmania and Victoria. Bakers and confectioners manufactured and sold their products on the premises, and samples of tea and coffee were given away.

Forty thousand cigars from the Philippines were on display. Students from the Victorian Asylum and School for the Blind gave demonstrations of brush-making and sold souvenirs to support their work. The timber resources of each Australian colony were displayed, and a highlight was a series of hand-painted wooden panels, prepared within Melbourne's Industrial and Technological Museum, showing the flowers and fruit of each type of timber represented.

Among the thousands of exhibitors in the Picture Gallery were some Australian artists, including Louis Buvelot, 'the Father of Australian landscape painting', and a group of younger Impressionists, including Tom Roberts, Frederick McCubbin and Arthur Streeton. This was a key moment in Australian art history, as Australian Impressionist paintings were displayed for a mass audience. The Victorian school system was demonstrated in three classrooms whose walls were covered with photographs of schools, pupils' drawings, maps and needlecraft. Educational exhibits from other Australian colonies, Great Britain and France allowed teachers to compare curricula and techniques. The Victorian court again demonstrated the quantity of gold discovered since 1851 and promoted the colony as a wonderful opportunity for investment in primary and secondary industries. A large-scale model of 'Early Melbourne, 1838' provided graphic evidence of how much the city had changed in a mere 50 years.

The exhibition was accompanied by an amazing musical festival, under the direction of an English conductor, Frederic Cowen, who was paid an astonishing 5000 pounds for six months work. He formed an orchestra and a choir of over 700 voices who gave more than 260 concerts – 10 concerts a week. The western transept of the Great Hall was converted to a concert hall with a false ceiling and moveable partitioning. Choir stalls were erected in tiers before the great organ that had been built by Melbourne organ builder George Fincham in 1880. Before the Centennial Exhibition, orchestral work had been almost unknown in Melbourne, and the musical program was thus exciting and eye-opening. Cowen gradually introduced modern pieces to the audience, and succeeded in expanding the city's musical taste. A poll towards the end of the series of concerts listed the most popular works: Beethoven's Pastoral Symphony, Wagner's overtures for *Tannhauser* and *Rienzi*, Handel's *Largo*, and Liszt's Hungarian Rhapsody No. 1.

Above: A number of cut, varnished and decorated timber samples were prepared within the Industrial and Technological Museum in Melbourne in 1885. May Vale illustrated the leaf and flower of each type of timber. This example shows red ironbark (*Eucalyptus sideroxylon*). The decorated timber samples were exhibited by the Victorian government in London, Adelaide, Melbourne and Paris between 1885 and 1889.
Museum Victoria Collection

Opposite: New South Wales showed off its mineral resources, but Victorian observers preferred their own court, with its emphasis on manufacturing industries. *Centennial International Exhibition, Official Record 1888–89.*
Museum Victoria Collection

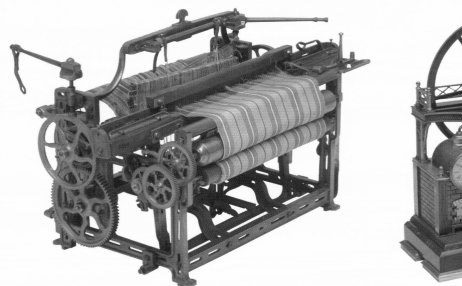

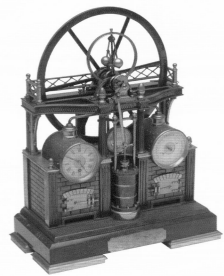

There was almost too much to see. Many visitors became disoriented in the large halls, and drifted aimlessly from one display to another. In a successful move to attract return visitors, the commissioners introduced a number of popular attractions, including a switch-back railway, an electric tramcar, roving conjurers and musicians and a shooting gallery. There were places to walk with a lover, away from the eyes of parents or chaperones; booths where lunches, tea and coffee were served, 'all flavoured with the holiday spirit, the bright talk of meeting friends'. After the exhibition closed in February 1889, Ada Cambridge wrote in mourning, 'When the place was shut at last, we wandered forlorn and lost for a long time. We were spoiled for humdrum life'.

Just over 2 million visits were made to the Centennial Exhibition, a figure nearly double the population of Victoria. But, despite this, it cost the Victorian government about a quarter of a million pounds. The commissioners tried to justify the expense by outlining the economic benefits which would flow to the colony. But the economic situation was changing, and within two years the boom had collapsed and Victorians were deserting the colony in search of jobs else-where. The Exhibition Building would not house such an extravagant event again. To quote Ada Cambridge again, 'The Exhibition marked the climax of the Boom, of what we erroneously called "the good times", when we were rich and dishonest and mercenary and vulgar'.

Opposite: This model of a double-hulled canoe from Manahiki, Cook Islands, was possibly included in the Centennial Exhibition. It is made from wood and pearl shell.
Museum Victoria Collection

Above left: Some displays at the exhibition gave a historical view of technological developments. The power loom revolutionised the production of cotton cloth. This model was shown at the Centennial Exhibition.
Museum Victoria Collection

Above right: This clock was presented to Rees Davies, the engineer responsible for works at the Exhibition Building in 1888, 'as a mark of respect and esteem'.
Museum Victoria Collection

UNITED 1901 ONE FLAG ONE HOPE

PERTH

ADELAIDE

MELBOURNE

SYDNEY

SANDS & McDOUGALL LTD

AUSTRALIAN COMMONWEALTH CELEBRATIONS.

THE GOVERNMENT OF VICTORIA requests the honor of th

Mr & Mrs Anthony Clota

at a Conversazione in the Exhibition Building on the Evening of Tuesday 7th May

4

The Building and the Nation

Twenty-one years after its opening, the Exhibition Building was again filled, for the opening of the first federal parliament on 9 May 1901. Parliamentary openings are generally held within the Parliament House, but in 1901 the prime minister, Edmund Barton, wanted the event to be 'a very great function' involving as many Australians as possible. The nation's largest building, the Exhibition Building, was therefore chosen, and 12 000 people were invited.

The Duke of Cornwall and York, the heir to the British throne, travelled from England to declare the parliament open. The royal visit confirmed Australia's links with Great Britain, and transformed a potentially dull political event into a grand ceremonial and festive occasion. All the major hotels were full, with dignitaries from all over Australia. The streets were decorated with arches, banners and flags. Thousands of people thronged into the city to admire the decorations and gaze at the illuminations by night. The *Age* reported general rejoicing 'even in the humble homes of the poor' where 'tiny twopenny flags ... a candle-lit kerosene tin punched with holes to form a crown or an outline map of Australia ... or a news-paper print of their Royal Highnesses before a candle' were displayed.

From early on the morning of 9 May, crowds began to make their way towards the Exhibition Building. The official guests were dressed soberly, the women in black

G. B. H. Austin, an architect within the Public Works Department, drew the building on his design for this invitation to a conversazione on 7 May 1901.
Museum Victoria Collection

Tom Roberts (1856–1931)
The Opening of Federal Parliament, 9 May 1901, 1903
Oil on canvas

Roberts wrote that his painting was 'A document?
Yes? And something more. The royalty and its suite of
Governors, of states and the members, democracy – with
the people – that's the Empire, and this all meets under
the one roof. And that's what I'm painting'.

or shades of lilac, because the court was still in mourning after the death of Queen Victoria in January. Only the occasional military uniform brightened the generally sombre effect. But there was great excitement at this, the birth of a united nation for a continent, the culmination of a long political process of negotiation, constitution making and referenda.

'The atmosphere was radiant and illuminated the vast spaces of the building and the great sea of faces with a bright Australian glow' wrote the *Argus* reporter. He went on to describe the gathering as '12 000 people seated in a vast amphitheatre – free people, hopeful people, courageous people – entrusted with working out their own destiny and rejoicing in their liberty'. He made special mention of the shaft of light that came through the clerestory windows just at the moment when the Duke declared parliament open. The crowd listened to speeches from the Duke and the Governor-General, sang a hymn and the national anthem, and watched as the new politicians were sworn in. They were filled with optimism and joy as they celebrated the making of the new nation.

Tom Roberts, who was to paint the occasion, described it in a letter to his son: 'So when the great day came your mother and I went to the hall of the Exhibition Building, and without getting seats walked quietly at the very back, and climbing up some rails, I was able to see that immense gathering of people from all over Australia, and from so many parts of the world. It was very solemn and great. The heads on the floor looked like a landscape stretching away'.

The celebrations continued for over a week. Politicians, community leaders, merchants, judges, clergy and their wives were caught up in a whirl of entertainment. Two days before the opening, the Victorian government hosted a conversazione, a reception with buffet food, music from a choir of 550 voices, champagne and Australian wines; the Exhibition Building was decorated with 'ropes of wheat-ears and poppies' for the occasion. Official guests were also invited to receptions at the Town Hall and Parliament House, a royal review at Flemington, and a demonstration by 10 000 state school children on the oval on the northern side of the building. There were processions galore – Sunday school children, trade unionists, stockmen, the Chinese community – and always crowds gathered to catch a glimpse of royalty as they rode by in the handsome state landau.

Julian and Howard Ashton were commissioned to design this invitation to a reception in the Exhibition Building on 9 May 1901.
Museum Victoria Collection

In May 1901, amateur photographer G. H. Myers captured the building lit up at night during the visit of the Duke and Duchess of Cornwall and York.

Museum Victoria Collection

On 9 May the new government hosted an evening reception in the Exhibition Building. The menu included turkey, duck and chicken, mutton, beef, ham, a boar's head, oysters, prawns and lobster, teal, iced asparagus and champagne jelly. Guests could drink 1893 Moët et Chandon champagne, wines from Germany, and Australian chablis, hock, claret, riesling, burgundy and tokay. Madame Nellie Stewart sang a hymn, *Australia*; works by Verdi and Wagner were played; and the evening ended with a dance. Well-known anarchist J. W. (Chummy) Fleming, who had led a demonstration by the unemployed as the royal couple arrived in Melbourne, thought the unemployed should be represented at the function. He entered undetected and spent over three hours mixing with the crowd before being quietly ejected.

A few days later, the Duchess of Cornwall and York visited the building again, this time to preside over a flag-raising ceremony. She pushed a button to send the message 'Hoist' by telegraph to 7000 schools throughout Australia and to London, New Zealand and Fiji. In some towns, fire bells were rung to signal to the school when the message was received. All over Australia, children gathered in their schoolyard and raised the Union Jack, cadet corps fired volleys into the air, speeches were made and the crowd joined in singing the national anthem, *God Save the King*. Some lucky children were given a half-holiday on the occasion.

An Englishman travelling with the royal couple wrote an 'open letter' to the people of Melbourne which was published in the press after they left. He expressed his appreciation for the opening celebrations: 'No event in recent times, to my knowledge, has been so magnificently staged before so huge an audience. The effect of numbers was stupendous, overwhelming … The evening receptions were on a gigantic scale too … Nowhere at home could one have seen full dress uniform side by side with tweed jackets at a state function, or a lady's evening dress flanked by a blouse and straw hat … Your nation is setting out towards its future independent of convention and habit'. This letter was much reproduced, and it told Australians what they wanted to hear. They were proud of making a new nation in a new land, a nation that would have strong links to Great Britain but that would have an independence and shape of its own.

After the royal couple had left Melbourne on their whistle-stop tour of the other Australian states, the new parliament met in the Victorian Parliament House. The displaced Victorian politicians grumblingly met in chambers in the western annexe to the Great Hall. They probably thought it would be a temporary arrangement, but it was not until 1927 that the federal parliament moved at last to the new national capital, Canberra, and the Victorian politicians could return to their building in Spring Street.

The Federation Decorative Scheme

In 1901 the interior of the Exhibition Building was redecorated in time for the opening of the first federal parliament. The decorative scheme was under the control of John Ross Anderson, who is also known for the interior design of the ANZ 'Gothic' Bank in Collins Street, Melbourne. It is his design we see today, after much restoration. The whole building, including the stencilled patterns on the walls and ceiling, was painted in 15 weeks by a team of 30 men.

Anderson chose a sober scheme in keeping with the solemnity and importance of the occasion. The great dome was painted to represent the sky. Underneath are four mottoes suitable for a new nation: *Dei gracia* – by the grace of God; *Carpe diem* – make the most of the day; *Aude sapere* – dare to be wise; and *Benigno numine* – with benign power. A frieze shows the products of industry and hints at the wealth of the new nation.

Maypole dancers in the state schools demonstration held at the Exhibition Building on 11 May 1901.

Museum Victoria Collection

Above: The sylph Summer
Source: Museum Victoria

Below: The sylph Justice
Source: Museum Victoria

On the arches are crescent-shaped lunettes representing Federation, Government, 'The Arts Applied to War' and 'The Arts Applied to Peace'. The image for Government shows the Roman goddess Minerva, representing Prudence, with Justice and Learning at her sides. The globe on the right depicts the countries of the British Empire in red, with Australia in a prominent position.

In 'The Arts Applied to Peace', Minerva reclines surrounded by symbols of peace: recreation, music, conversation and artistic endeavour. Minerva is associated with the arts and wisdom. The sleeping lion at her feet represents the might of the British Empire, resting in peacetime, but at hand when needed.

Britannia rides in her chariot of war in 'The Arts Applied to War'. The Australian states are depicted as amazons, armed and following her into battle. They are accompanied by cherubs, also carrying bows and arrows. The Federation image shows Britannia welcoming the federated states who carry their heraldic shields. She joins their hands in union. From left we see South Australia, Tasmania, Western Australia, New South Wales, Britannia, Victoria and Queensland. Cherubs and an angel sing and dance for joy at the peaceful birth of the new nation.

Below the lunettes, eight women in draped costumes and known as sylphs, represent Truth, Justice, Night, Day, and the four seasons. Allegorical figures, usually women, were widely used at this time to represent nations, values, stories or themes. In 1901 many people would have immediately recognised their symbolic associations. All the figured work was done by Gordon Coutts, George Dancey, Girolamo Nerli and Leon Pole. According to a contemporary newspaper report, the artists had originally supplied the sylphs with less clothing than they have today. On viewing the work, the trustees, 'gravely shaking their heads, insisted on the figures being shimmered over with more drapery'.

Around the dome are plaster heads which were part of the first decorative scheme of 1880. They represent people from all the continents, and they include an Indigenous Australian, a Chinese man, and an Indian. There is irony in the thought that these figures overlooked the first hours of that parliament which quickly instituted the policy of restrictive immigration that became known as the White Australia Policy.

The decorative scheme which can be seen today is essentially that designed in 1901. It was restored in 1994 under the direction of Allom Lovell Sanderson Pty

Ltd, conservation architects. As part of the restoration, 10 500 hand-stencilled rosettes were applied to the walls and ceiling.

The Australian Flag

The Exhibition Building is the place where the Australian flag was flown for the first time. At Federation, Australia had no national flag. An unofficial Federation Flag (a blue cross with the Southern Cross on a white background) was flown with Great Britain's Union Jack during the celebrations.

Above left: 'The Arts Applied to Peace'
Photographer: James Lauritz
Source: Museum Victoria

Above right: 'The Arts Applied to War'
Photographer: James Lauritz
Source: Museum Victoria

Below left: The pendentive figure Venus
Source: Museum Victoria

Below right: The pendentive figure Hercules
Source: Museum Victoria

This was probably one of the designs submitted to the competition for an Australian flag.

Museum Victoria Collection

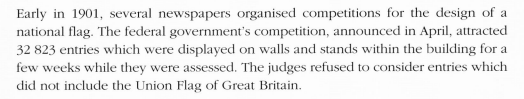

Early in 1901, several newspapers organised competitions for the design of a national flag. The federal government's competition, announced in April, attracted 32 823 entries which were displayed on walls and stands within the building for a few weeks while they were assessed. The judges refused to consider entries which did not include the Union Flag of Great Britain.

Five entrants who produced similar designs shared the prize money. Their design forms the basis for our current flag. Originally, the large Federation Star had six points, one for each state. Later another point was added to represent the Australian territories. On 3 September 1901, the Countess of Hopetoun, the wife of the Governor-General, announced the winners and unfurled the new flag.

A Nation's Portrait

For early twentieth-century Australians, Charles Nuttall's painting of the opening of federal parliament was *the* image that represented the moment when the nation was created. Its scale (it is over 4 metres long) helped convey the grandeur and formality of the event, but the image was best known through smaller reproductions that were hung in homes and public places.

This is one of a series of plaster representations of the peoples of the world, incorporated into the building's first decorative scheme in 1880 and still visible.

Source: Museum Victoria

Nuttall, an etcher and illustrator, was commissioned to produce a painting that would be worthy of the occasion. He set up a studio in the Exhibition Building, and chose to paint the moment when the sun streamed through the windows as the Duke declared parliament open. He travelled extensively to sketch from life many of the public figures who appear in the painting.

Reproductions of the painting were presented by groups of citizens to schools, lodges and libraries throughout Australia. Countless speeches expressed the view that the image would 'inspire the spirit of patriotism … true loyalty … and national unity'. But the painting's life as an icon was a short one. After the First World War, depictions of the war and especially of Gallipoli became the great national images. Nuttall's painting lapsed into obscurity and was relegated to a damp basement in the Exhibition Building. It was restored in 1984 and became part of Museum Victoria's Collection in 1996. It can now be seen hanging on the north side of the mezzanine of the Royal Exhibition Building.

The War Museum

Another chapter of national significance for the Exhibition Building occurred in 1922, when the first displays of the Australian War Museum opened in the eastern annexe to the Great Hall. Sixty thousand young Australians had died on the battle-fields of Turkey, Egypt, France and Belgium, and the Museum was established as part of the national process of memorialising and grieving.

The exhibits emphasised the experience of the individual soldier, the conditions of battle and the equipment used. There were displays of guns, uniforms, aeroplanes, documents, specially commissioned paintings of the battle scenes, and souvenirs collected by soldiers on the battlefields. A highlight was a series of large dioramas showing the terrain of some of the major Australian battles. Returned servicemen brought their mothers, or the mothers of dead comrades, and pored over the models to trace the actions in which they had been involved. For many it was a cathartic experience. The *Herald*'s reporter suggested that 'Parents of fallen men will go in grief and come away in pride'.

Charles Nuttall (1872–1934)
*The Opening of the
First Federal Parliament,
9 May 1901,* 1902
Oil on canvas

Museum Victoria Collection

Above: Part of the aircraft
collection on display at the
Exhibition Building, 1922.

Source: Australian War Memorial

Below: Cover of the first
catalogue of the collection of the
Australian War Museum, 1922.

Museum Victoria Collection

Almost 800 000 people visited the exhibition in Melbourne over the next three years. In 1923, the Museum became the Australian War Memorial. The exhibition moved to Sydney in April 1925, but the Memorial's staff and most of the collection remained in Melbourne until 1935, when plans for the permanent building in Canberra had progressed. When the foundations for Melbourne Museum were being dug in 1997, excavators found a couple of rusty cannon from the First World War, discarded by War Memorial staff on their move to Canberra.

A Military Barracks

During the Second World War, the building was largely given over to technicians from the Royal Australian Air Force who were accommodated there while they were trained in wireless mechanics, instrument making and other trades. Up to 700 men slept in the Great Hall. Jack Baskerville recalls: 'I will never forget the straw palliasse on the bare floor boards on the balcony overlooking the main hall of the Exhibition Building. Thank God we arrived early in the year when it was not too cold. Later, of course, it was pure torture for a north Queenslander to suffer his first Melbourne winter. I recall showers which seemed a mile away from our bunks, the long queue for the basins and the showers, the even longer line up of bare bums, all shapes and sizes. Not even a female one among them to add a bit of spice. Then there was the piano on the stage there and the wartime songs. I even recall Tchaikovsky's No. 1 Piano Concerto floating up. And there was the unforgettable marching to and from the technical college'.

Doug Brooke described his training in 1942: 'What would life at the Exhibition Building have been like without the "Midnight Stalker" and empty rubbish bins mysteriously rolling down stairs and thundering throughout that enormous space. Followed, of course, by the noise from many airmen awakened from their sleep'. Other men recall being kept awake by the noise of the seals from the Aquarium, and hating the loud 'hooters' suspended from the dome that sounded for reveille, breakfast, morning and midday parades, evening meal and lights out. Access to the building was prohibited between midnight and 6 a.m., but airmen found many ingenious ways to avoid the guards and clamber in.

When the floor of the Great Hall was replaced in 1985, workers discovered a wide variety of ephemeral items that had been left behind by airmen and had slipped between the floor boards. They included cigarette and chocolate wrappers, condom packets, leave passes, theatre tickets and personal correspondence.

Above: During the Second World War, the area to the north of the building was dug for trenches, in case of aerial attack. These RAAF mechanics formed the champion trench-digging team in 1942.
Museum Victoria Collection

Below: Some of the items left behind when the RAAF moved out at the end of the war are now in Museum Victoria's Collection.
Source: Museum Victoria

A Cathedral of Commerce

5

Throughout its history, the Exhibition Building has provided opportunities for local and international manufacturers to display their products. New inventions, locally patented goods, models of machines and demonstrations of new techniques were regularly displayed, integral parts of a great variety of industrial, technical and trade exhibitions. These continued to be held in the building until 1996 when the larger Melbourne Exhibition Centre opened at Southbank.

During the first half of the twentieth century, Victorian manufacturers expanded into new industrial estates, in the western and northern suburbs and in some country centres. In a series of 'All-Australian Exhibitions', companies like Dunlop (rubber goods ranging from rugs to golf balls to brake couplings), Sands and MacDougall (stationery), Henry Buck and Company (shirt and pyjama making) and the Broken Hill Proprietary Company ('steel bars, channels, fish plates, beams, pig iron, pig lead, blocks of zinc, billets and blooms') showed their products to great crowds. Local businessmen were confident that they could produce as well and as cheaply as their overseas competitors.

Trade exhibitions had an educative as well as a commercial role. In 1913 the Australian Manufactures and Hygiene Exhibition run by the Australian Natives' Association included displays on public health. There were exhibits on the control

At the 1963 Motor Show, family cars from Britain dominated this section of the display. Visitors to the show could also see Jack Brabham's racing car, a Rolls-Royce Silver Cloud, and displays promoting the use of seat belts.

Photographer: Edwin G. Adamson
Museum Victoria Collection

Between 1905 and 1926, the Australian Natives' Association sponsored 10 exhibitions that promoted Australian products. This is the cover of the 1908 exhibition program.

Museum Victoria Collection

of flies, what clothing was suitable for Australian conditions, the prevention of tuberculosis, and the control of venereal disease. There was also a 'model kitchen, pantry and laundry, fitted on hygienic lines'. This promoted safety in the home, with good ventilation, fly screens, large jugs that could be easily cleaned, hot and cold water in the kitchen, good air circulation around fruit and vegetables, and sliding doors to cupboards. Such displays aimed to improve health in the home; the organisers considered that Victorian mothers were not yet aware of the benefit of fresh air, unrestrictive clothing and good nutrition for young children.

By the 1930s, the 'Palace of Industry' had metamorphosed into a 'A Cathedral of Commerce'. Visitors still went to the Exhibition Building to marvel at the newest inventions. But now it was not only what was new that was on display, but also what was fashionable, and many of the newest things were becoming accessible and affordable. Exhibitions became 'bazaars' where skilled salesmen promoted their goods and tried to persuade the visitor that the latest consumer goods were really necessities.

Home Shows were among the most popular exhibitions. They were first held in 1936 and reached the height of popularity in the 1950s and 1960s, as new generations of Melburnians established homes in the suburbs. Visitors who came to the Red Cross Home Show in 1949 were urged to 'see the thousands of practical modern ideas and appliances for your home of tomorrow'. They could see a home designed by architect Robin Boyd, erected on the balcony near the organ and taking advantage of the sloping choir stalls. His 'House of Tomorrow', valued at 3000 pounds, with its timber frame, flat roof, large windows and cantilevered second floor, was 'the exemplar of good taste and Modern style'. Boyd fitted out the house with the latest in Australian design: Grant Featherston furniture, Frances Burke fabrics, Beco lighting, and ceramics by Arthur Merric Boyd. A new feature was a galley kitchen attached to the dining room. One visitor suggested that it was 'more of a dream house from the screen; the average working man would be afraid to invest without knowledge of its proof against weather, wear and time', yet he conceded that it was 'light, spacious, attractive and comfortable'.

At the 1951 Jubilee Exhibition, the 'Canberra' dining room suite, 'styled along Scandinavian lines, redesigned to suit Australian tastes' and constructed from Queensland walnut, was on display: it included a table and six chairs, a buffet and a cocktail cabinet. The bright green Semak Vitamizer was for sale, as well as the new waterproof Elastoplasts. For the back garden, Hill's rotary clothes hoists were on display for the first time. The architectural profession was trying to promote new designs to the growing market of home purchasers; they showed an 'H-shaped' home, 'the Sunshine House', selected from hundreds of plans available through the profession's Small Homes Service. It featured a separate sleeping and living wing, simple construction techniques, the use of bright colours and protection from the sun. 'In short', wrote Robin Boyd, 'there is no nonsense about it.' In a defensive mode, architect Neil Clerehan wrote in the exhibition catalogue: 'Another contemporary house is built. Almost certainly it will be regarded by neighbours with undisguised amazement and scorn. That is the price the occupants must pay for living in a contemporary house in Melbourne'.

In 1957, 180 000 people visited the Homes Exhibition. The advertisers were delighted, suggesting that 'the public of Melbourne has accepted this exhibition as the most convenient, the most thorough means of obtaining their requirements, whether it be for building, re-equipping or adding to their homes'. At this exhibition, no less than four complete homes were on display. Television was new in Melbourne, and the organisers provided seating so that visitors could watch TV and compare Australian-made and imported models. There was also a 'massive food display' that provided many Victorians with their first opportunity to experience the delights of supermarket shopping; with its tasting booths and give-away samples, the supermarket on the gallery had 'a carnival atmosphere'.

Motor Shows, where the latest model cars and motorcycles were on show, were also popular events. Victorians were enthusiastic purchasers of the new motorised transport from the very first. At least four local companies – the Australasian Horseless Carriage Syndicate (1897), Herbert Thomson of Armadale (1898), Tarrant and Lewis (1899) and Haines and Grut (1909) – made cars, but they could not compete with imported British and European cars like Argylls, De Dions, Mercedes and Talbots. After 1909, the Ford Model T began to be imported from America; this was the first car sold at a price that made it a serious rival to the horse and buggy, and demand increased even further.

The 1912 Victorian Motor Show was the first held in the building. The reporter from the *Argus,* in a passage reminiscent of the pride and belief in progress of

Exterior view of architect Robin Boyd's 'House of Tomorrow', which was erected in the organ gallery during the Home Show of 1949.

Photographer: Wolfgang Sievers
Source: Powerhouse Museum

30 years before, praised the 160 000 pounds worth of motor cars on show, 'polished, gleaming with brass and nickel … all this speed and power and mechanical perfection arose from nothing in the short space of about twelve years. [Then] there was not a motor-car in Melbourne, except the steam car built by Mr Thomson'. In a rather unfortunate allusion, he went on to say '[Now] we have a difference about as pronounced as that between Noah's Ark and a sailing clipper, certainly as great as that between Fuller's first steam boat and the Titanic'. The show was a great success, attracting 36 000 visitors, and most of the cars on display were sold before it closed.

Motor Shows during the 1920s and 1930s were lavish events, complete with brass band entertainment, lounge bars and dining rooms, motorbike races, and a special section for women motorists, 'The Creche', where 'light' and 'baby' cars were displayed. Motor writers excelled in the use of sensual prose. In 1929, one wrote of the 'sleek bodies of lavish limousines, rakish looking roadsters, sedate sedans and bonny little "babies" basking luxuriously in the glitter of a thousand electric lights and throwing back the reflection in scintillating gleams'. At later shows, dealers employed young women, often scantily dressed, to pose with the new cars and to attract the eye of potential purchasers.

It was not until 1948 that Australia had its own mass-produced car for the home market. At the Motor Show in 1949, the new Holden was on display, but demand was so great that purchasers had to wait two and a half years before their new car could be delivered. (On the other hand, a new Rolls Royce could be delivered immediately, at about eight times the cost!) Over 230 000 visitors admired the new cars in 1949, but most could not afford to buy them outright. Styles continued to change. The motor press dubbed 1958 'the year of the fins', after enormous American cars like the Dodge, Plymouth, and Chrysler Royal made an appearance. By 1965, small cars – the locally made Morris 850, the Volkswagen Beetle and the Mini Minor – were making an impact. During the 1970s, Ford promoted its own pop group, 'The Going Thing', who performed during the show, while General Motors Holden displayed a purple 'hot-rod' utility to attract young men and their girlfriends, the car buyers of the future.

Cars were not the only things that fired the imaginations of Melbourne's consumers. As Australians became wealthier and had more leisure time, the building hosted a range of specialist exhibitions appealing to those with money to spend and leisure to spend it in. Travel shows, caravanning and camping shows, exhibitions for backpackers, displays of demountable holiday homes, motorbike and yachting shows: all attracted large audiences who dreamed of what could be and purchased to fulfil their dreams.

Perhaps the clearest evidence of the relationship between dreams and commerce comes from Melbourne's Flower and Garden Show, still held every autumn. The building and the surrounding garden are transformed as the latest plants, the newest cultivars and the smartest garden accessories go on show. Exhibitors also present the latest overseas trends, encouraging the suburban gardener to redesign the home garden in response. The increasing domination of garden design by professionals is changing the face of the suburbs as consumers upgrade to keep up with the latest fashion. The Exhibition Building continues to retain its role as a 'Cathedral of Commerce'.

America comes to Melbourne. This model was promoting an American vehicle at the 1971 International Motor Show.
Photographer: Laurie Richards
Museum Victoria Collection

A Meeting Place

6

The Exhibition Building has always been a magnet for the people of Melbourne. It has been a place of entertainment and enjoyment where you could join with crowds of friends and strangers to visit an exhibition, to shop, to while away a wet afternoon at the Museum or Aquarium, or to experience the thrill of a fast-moving sporting event. The promenade in front of the building has been a favourite place for a Sunday morning walk after church, and generations of students have endured university exams in the draughty Great Hall, meeting outside afterwards to compare notes and head off to Carlton to drown their sorrows.

For many years, the Exhibition Building was the largest building in Melbourne. Even though the interior acoustics were appalling, it was the natural venue for large public gatherings. In September 1891 the founder of the Salvation Army, General William Booth, visited Melbourne and spoke to 6000 people who had waited over two hours to hear him. The *Illustrated Australian News* reported that 'his triumphant procession through the streets and reception at the Exhibition Building were absolutely without a parallel in the way of spontaneous enthusiasm'. On the next day, a Sunday, he addressed over 21 000 people, in three sessions, with two huge meetings on the following evenings. During this visit he outlined the Army's plan to train slum-dwellers from 'Darkest England' and bring them to Australia where, the Army believed, they would have greater economic and social opportunities.

Crowds packed the building in May 1912 to hear American evangelist John Wilbur Chapman. *Australasian*, 25 May 1912.
Source: State Library of Victoria

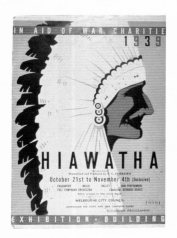

The program cover for the cantata *Hiawatha*, by Samuel Coleridge-Taylor, performed in the building in 1939.

Museum Victoria Collection

In 1912, American evangelists John Wilbur Chapman and Charles Alexander filled the building, with crowds of 15 000 packing the balconies and relishing the preaching, the appeals to conversion, and the new hymns with choruses and catchy tunes. A more sombre note was set in 1950 when a packed audience at the Australian Peace Congress heard the Anglican Dean of Canterbury, Dr Hewlett Johnson, the 'Red Dean', warn of the dangers of nuclear war and defend the intentions of Stalin's Russia. This was the last time such a controversial speech was given in the building. The chairman of trustees declared afterwards that 'no body which makes traitorous and disloyal utterances will ever get in the building while I am a trustee'. More recently, a Roman Catholic Archbishop of Melbourne, George Pell, was inducted at a ceremony in the building because St Patrick's Cathedral was undergoing restoration at the time.

In the last 40 years, the coming of television and the growing popularity of marches and political demonstrations have lessened the demand for a large space where people can meet to hear a special speaker, but the building is still used for public meetings by organisations that expect to attract a crowd of 10 000 or more. Modern sound systems can overcome the acoustic deficiencies, and the interior space can be made flexible by the use of screens.

Until the Concert Hall was opened in 1982, the Melbourne Town Hall was the main concert venue for the city, but artists who could attract large crowds sometimes performed in the Exhibition Building. Dame Nellie Melba sang to nearly 9000 people in 1907; the organisers overcame some of the acoustic problems by spreading sawdust under the galleries and placing a huge sounding board over the south transept. All types of concerts have been held in the building. The Melbourne Symphony Orchestra and the Philharmonic Choir, augmented by 1500 school children, performed with three soloists for the Australian Sick and Wounded Soldiers Fund in September 1915, and other charitable bodies organised entertainments during the First World War. In 1939, on the outbreak of another war, the Red Cross and War Comforts Fund benefited from a 15-day season of the cantata *Hiawatha*, which had a chorus of 700, no fewer than 80 ballet dancers, and a full symphony orchestra conducted by Bernard Heinze. Musical events here have always had a unique feel. During 2001, as a special event for the centenary of Federation, Mahler's Eighth Symphony, the *Symphony of a Thousand*, was performed to a gala audience. In March 2003, amplified music at a Moby concert shook the rafters, dislodging dust from between the ceiling boards over the enthusiastic audience.

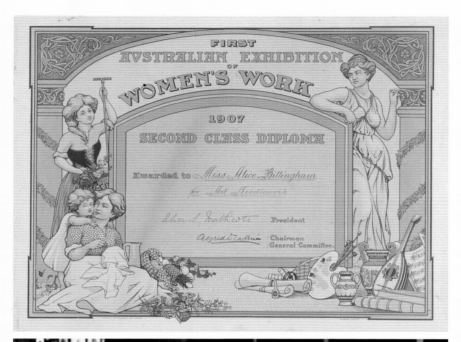

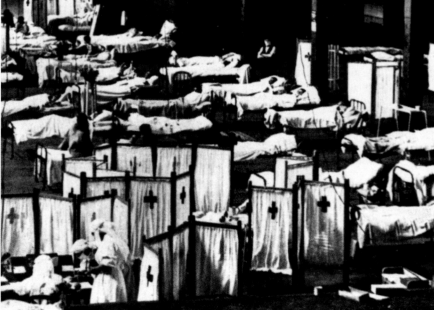

Above: In 1907 a well-attended exhibition of women's work was held in the building. This certificate was awarded for a drawn-thread tablecloth.

Museum Victoria Collection

Below: In 1919 the building became a temporary fever hospital, where some of the hundreds of Melburnians who caught the Spanish influenza were cared for. *Melbourne Punch*, 13 February 1919.

Source: State Library of Victoria

Charity bazaars have often been held in the building. The Grand National Baby Show was held in 1893. There were 700 babies under two, and there was bedlam as they were inspected, prodded and criticised by an audience of nearly 30 000. A reporter from the *Weekly Times* took a special interest in an Aboriginal baby from Corranderrk mission, near Healesville, whose mother 'sat complacently facing the wondering, laughing crowd, fully appreciating the fact that she and her stalwart spouse and dusky son were the centre of attention'.

The world's first six-day penny-farthing bicycle race was held inside the building in 1882. Ten years later, a tug-of-war competition between teams of 'ladies' attracted much controversy. The *Argus* claimed that 'a public building was never put to a more degrading use', but a crowd of 3000 men cheered the young women on. A variety of other sporting events has been held within and around the building. Cycle races, hot-air balloon ascents, firefighting demonstrations, motor-bike racing and demonstrations by school cadets have all attracted crowds. The exhibition oval, on the north side of the building, was a popular venue for many decades, and the site of speedway cycle races for eight years after 1928. During the Melbourne Olympics in 1956, the Great Hall was set aside for the weightlifting and wrestling competitions, and a special annexe was built for the basketball competition.

After the Second World War, the Commonwealth government rented the Exhibition oval and constructed nearly 30 timber-framed bungalows to serve as short-term accommodation for the stream of newly-arrived migrants to Victoria. They were expected to stay only a few days while they organised employment and more permanent accommodation. Some remember feeling cold as the bungalows had no heating; others recall being eaten by mosquitoes on hot summer nights; all were relieved when they moved out to begin their 'real' life in Australia.

The Great Hall and its annexes have seen the beginning of many romances, and the ending of not a few. The first Exhibition dance hall was known as the Palais Royale, and nicknamed 'the home of disappointed lovers'. A new generation of young people was attracted to the pink, green and white Royale Ballroom which, on its opening in April 1952, was 'the most modern in the southern hemisphere' and the only air-conditioned ballroom in Australia. It remained a popular meeting place for fifteen years; it was renovated in 1968 and demolished in 1979. Regular discos, dinners and formal balls continue to be held in the Great Hall, which can accommodate over 2000 people for a sit-down banquet.

Above: The crowd at the
Moby concert, March 2003.
Source: Museum Victoria

Below: Each year the Exhibition
Building shines during the Flower
and Garden Show.
Source: Museum Victoria

Above: Seals perform outside the Aquarium behind the Exhibition Building. *Argus*, 21 January 1933.

Source: Museum Victoria

Below: An advertisement for 'The Victorian South Kensington'. *Argus*, 26 September 1892.

Source: State Library of Victoria

In May 2001, a series of great gatherings were held to commemorate the centenary of Federation. Politicians, community leaders and prominent citizens met together to celebrate 'A Nation United'. The events were televised and the Royal Exhibition Building was once again the focus of national attention. The building will remain an exciting venue for large events, and it has a continuing future as a meeting place.

The Museum, Art Gallery and Aquarium

In 1885, the trustees opened an Aquarium, Picture Gallery and Museum in a building behind the eastern annexe. This was a world of wonders, packed with exotic sights. The Museum had courts for zoology, botany, ethnology, mineralogy and entomology, as well as fisheries and armaments displays. There were two Egyptian mummies, and the iron armour worn by a member of the Kelly gang. There was also a planetarium and a children's theatre where the walls were painted with nursery rhymes. Moving pictures were shown from 1909.

THE VICTORIAN "SOUTH KENSINGTON."
What You Can See for ONE SHILLING.

THE AQUARIUM, with Living Seals, who feed and perform at 3 o'clock, Man-Eating Crocodiles, Tortoises, and Aquatic Birds.

FERNERY, Living Fountains, and Waterfalls.

CYCLORAMA, Melbourne, 1841, painted from authentic drawings by Mr. J. Hennings.

THE GOLDSEEKER, Realistic Bush Scene, with full-sized Aboriginals, Gin, and Children.

The FINE ART GALLERY, Pictures, Antiques, &c.

MUSEUMS—Ethnological, Anthropological, Mineralogical, Conchological, Entomological. Costumes and Weapons of War of Ancient and Modern Nations.

ST. PETER'S at ROME, Magnificent Model, with Clerical Processions, &c.

MANUFACTURES and PRODUCTS, obtained by the Trustees from all Countries.

Admission to the Whole Collection, 1s.; Children, 6d.

The Cyclorama of Early Melbourne, 38 metres long and four metres tall, occupied a large circular room within the Museum. Cycloramas were 360 degree illusionist paintings, viewed from above from a tall central platform. The Exhibition cyclorama was a panoramic picture of central Melbourne painted from an 1841 sketch that Samuel Jackson had made from the roof of the first Scots Church in Collins Street. Once visitors had viewed the cyclorama, they were urged to climb to the dome to see how Melbourne had changed.

The Aquarium, the first in Australia, displayed crocodiles, seals, penguins from the Antarctic and fish from all over the world. Feeding time at 3 p.m. was a great attraction. Visitors could also explore a fernery, with monkeys and exotic birds. There were weapons from Indigenous Australians, and a collection of narrative paintings, mostly of little value, lent by the trustees or left behind after the international exhibitions. Melburnians were saddened when the Aquarium was destroyed by fire in 1953. The fish, most of the Museum exhibits and the records of the trustees went up in the blaze.

Part of the Cyclorama of Early Melbourne, painted on canvas by John Hennings in 1892 from an 1841 sketch by Samuel Jackson, and on display in the Exhibition Museum for over 40 years. It was badly damaged by water when the Aquarium burnt down in 1953, but survives in the collection of the State Library of Victoria.

Photograph: Museum Victoria

Epilogue Restoring the Building

After the Second World War, the building remained in use for regular trade fairs, but the trustees did not spend much money on it. It began to be spoken of as a white elephant, and lost some favour. In 1948 the Melbourne City Council debated a proposal that it be demolished and that government offices be built on the site. The proposition was lost by only one vote.

About 1954, Trevor Riddell began to organise exhibitions in Melbourne. He recalled: 'In those days the Exhibition Building was in a shocking state of repair. It was riddled with white ants. Its wooden kitchen was the greatest fire risk in Melbourne, apart from the building itself. Three foot logs were used to cook food and the smoke just billowed out through the dining room and into the exhibition hall. It needed painting. The floors were bad. We really had to dress it up to make the place look attractive … The first exhibition I did up there I got lost. You'd go into some rooms and there'd be a dead end. Parts had been boarded up for the hospital and for the air force during the war. There were rats and possums. Upstairs they had Ned Kelly's armour. Nobody wanted it'.

Despite its dilapidated state, the building continued to be used, and repairs were done as the money became available. The trustees created car parks on the west and south of the building. The back of the site was a mish-mash of demountable buildings, many of which had been built for the migrant reception centre after the Second World War. These were gradually demolished as the need for them decreased. The enlarged car parks brought in additional funds. The 1880 western annexe, for so long the site of the Victorian parliament and then the home of the Country Roads Board and other gov-

ernment departments, was demolished in the 1960s. The eastern annexe was demolished in 1979 and replaced with a new exhibition area, Centennial Hall, with its controversial mirrored façade.

In 1975 the Exhibition Building was included in the Australian Heritage Commission's Register of the National Estate. At first the trustees resisted any attempts by government bodies to impose heritage controls over the building. Eventually, however, they commissioned a heritage architect, Allan Willingham, to prepare a conservation analysis of the Great Hall. His 1983 report painted a gloomy picture: 'The dome was in a dilapidated condition, with many slates dislodged. Some of the cast iron ventilators were hanging precariously, and even the lantern structure had decayed. The timber ring bands supporting the dome's timber framework were structurally suspect and the hidden roof gutters had rusted out … Many of the clerestory windows along the naves and galleries were leaking'.

The first part of the repair was a new floor: the old baltic pine was replaced with Queensland cypress pine between 1985 and 1989. (This floor is gradually being replaced with spotted gum.) A concrete service tunnel in the basement now supplies electricity, telephone, gas and plumbing to the exhibitors in the Great Hall. Next, the roof needed urgent attention. In 1988, a cast iron finial from the decking around the dome collapsed, falling through the roof and embedding itself in the floor. This incident, which occurred only days after the hall was filled to capacity for a concert to celebrate the bicentennial of European settlement of Australia, spurred the trustees on to a structural restoration, which led to a new roof, new slates and timber in the dome, and restored windows. The lantern at the top of the dome has been re-gilded with 22ct gold leaf, and the 160 urns on the exterior have been repaired or replaced. The gasoliers inside the building are interpretations of those installed in 1888; they are in fact run by electricity.

Once the decision was made to restore the interior decoration of the building, many layers of grey, pink and cream paint were laboriously removed to reveal traces of the schemes of 1880, 1888 and 1901. The restoration was based on the 1901 scheme, as there was substantial documentary evidence for it: good photographs exist, and the designer's original cartoons have survived. The work was supervised by Robyn Riddett, of conservation architects Allom Lovell Sanderson Pty Ltd. Over 160 shades have been identified in the decorative scheme, and these have been carefully reproduced.

Work was also done on the sylphs, the eight female figures; the pendentives or the four figures of Mars, Venus, Mercury and Hercules; and the 'extradoses' or the alle-gorical paintings at the top of each side of the dome. These were very dirty, and the canvas on which they had been painted had stretched and become brittle over time. Layers of varnish were removed, canvas and plaster were patched, the drawings were cleaned, and damaged or missing pieces were replaced.

In 1998, after Museum Victoria was given responsibility for the building, repairs were done to the northern façade and it was repainted externally after remaining annexes were demolished. But a large building like this is continually changing and decaying, and repairs and restoration will continue to be required.

World Heritage Nomination

In 2003, the Federal Minister for the Environment and Heritage announced that the Royal Exhibition Building and Carlton Gardens will be assessed for World Heritage listing. His announcement continued: 'The Royal Exhibition Building, set in Melbourne's Carlton Gardens, is one of the world's great enduring monuments to the International Exhibition movement of the late nineteenth and early twentieth centuries, which expressed the confidence and expansion of the Industrial Age. The Building, in its garden setting, is one of the last tangible, symbolic representations of this significant historical period. World Heritage listing of this extraordinary place would for the first time recognise post-European settlement and built heritage as part of Australia's rich and internationally important heritage'.

The allegorical painting 'The Arts Applied to Peace', partly cleaned and patched.

Photograph: Victorian Centre for the Conservation of Cultural Material Inc.
Source: Museum Victoria

Further Reading

Colligan, Mimi. *Canvas Documentaries: Panoramic Entertainments in Nineteenth Century Australia and New Zealand*. Carlton, Victoria, Melbourne University Press, 2002

Davison, Graeme. 'Exhibitions', *Australian Cultural History,* no. 2, 1982–83, pp. 5–21

Dunstan, David (ed.) *Victorian Icon: The Royal Exhibition Building, Melbourne*. Kew, Victoria, Exhibition Trustees in association with Australian Scholarly Publishing, 1996

Hoffenberg, Peter H. *An Empire on Display: English, Indian and Australian Exhibitions from the Crystal Palace to the Great War*. Berkeley, University of California Press, 2001

Lane, Terence. 'European ceramics at the 1880-81 Melbourne International Exhibition', *Australian Antique and Fine Art Dealers' Fair, catalogue, Melbourne, 23–27 October 1996,* pp. 9–15

Parris, John and Shaw, A. G. L. 'The Melbourne International Exhibition 1880–1881', *Victorian Historical Journal,* vol. 51, no. 4, 1980, pp. 237–54

Riddett, Robyn. '*Carpe Diem* and the exhibition of enterprise!', *Australian Antique and Fine Art Dealers' Fair, catalogue, Melbourne, 26–29 October 1995,* pp. 18–23

Sharples, John. 'Medals of the Melbourne International Exhibitions', *Australian Antique and Fine Art Dealers' Fair, catalogue, Melbourne, 23–27 October 1996,* pp. 16–21

'Victoria at the Great Exhibitions, 1851–1900', *La Trobe Library Journal,* 14, no. 56, 1995 (whole issue)

Whitehead, Georgina. *Civilising the City: A History of Melbourne's Public Gardens*. Melbourne, State Library of Victoria, 1997

Willis, Elizabeth. 'Souvenirs from the great Melbourne Exhibitions', *Australian Antique and Fine Art Dealers' Fair, catalogue, Melbourne, 23–27 October 1996,* pp. 5–8

Acknowledgments

I wish to acknowledge my debt to previous writers on the Royal Exhibition Building, in particular David Dunstan and the other contributors to *Victorian Icon: The Royal Exhibition Building, Melbourne*.

I would also like to thank the team of volunteers who have worked over many years to gather documentary and graphic material to illustrate the story of the building. Thanks especially to Ken Green and Fay Baker, Ivy Raadik, Elizabeth Hebb and Bill Woodward for maintaining the files and databases of the REB collection at Museum Victoria, which has been and remains an invaluable resource.

Thank you too to the many people and organisations who have assisted the production of this book. To my colleagues at Museum Victoria, in the Australian Society and Technology Department, in the Production Studio, Design and across the organisation, thank you.

 Elizabeth Willis is a Senior Curator in the Australian Society and Technology Department, Museum Victoria.

Museum Victoria gratefully acknowledges the support of Arts Victoria for providing funding towards this publication.

Photography Credits

Jonathon Augier, page 51 (Flower and Garden Show)
John Broomfield, pages 4, 26, 27, 34, 35, (sylphs and pendentive figures) 36, 53
Frank Coffa, page 1
Benjamin Healley, pages 51 (Moby concert), 56
Michelle McFarlane, pages 11, 16, 17, 36 (flag)